THE
Archive Photographs
SERIES

SELBY

FROM THE

WILLIAM RAWLING COLLECTION

The Selby Abbey and the Town Coat of Arms. According to legend a monk from the founding town of Auxerre had a vision of a river bend, three swans and suitable ground to build an Abbey. Having received his architectural plans from above, the monk set off for England and arrived at Salisbury; the site seemed suitable and there was a definite bend in the local river but the three required fowl failed to emerge. The monk moved north to a bend in the Ouse whereupon three swans dutifully appeared and the site for the Abbey (at Church Hill) was established.

THE
Archive Photographs
SERIES

SELBY

FROM THE

WILLIAM RAWLING COLLECTION

Compiled by
Matthew Young

CHALFORD

First published 1995
Copyright © Matthew Young, 1995

The Chalford Publishing Company
St Mary's Mill, Chalford,
Stroud, Gloucestershire, GL6 8NX

ISBN 0 7524 0198 X

Typesetting and origination by
The Chalford Publishing Company
Printed in Great Britain by
Redwood Books, Trowbridge

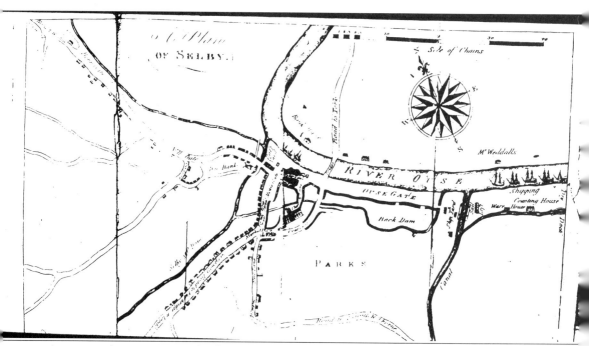

A nineteenth century map of Selby.

Contents

William Rawling was a Selby photographer, Master of the Blue Coat School, Secretary to the Freemasons and a local saddler. His photographs form part of the collection donated by his descendant Doctor Morley in 1960 to the Yorkshire Archaeological Society. He was a singer with the Abbey Choir and local Journalist Addison Towse described his voice as like 'heavy artillery – a thirty-two foot grand organ pedal'. His career as a teacher was less successful as an inspection of the Blue Coat School in 1867 by Martin stated that: 'the dress [of the school] is hideous and absurd. The master approves of all except the cap. The clothes don't last a year and become very ragged … '. Later comments state: 'The Master is Mr Rawling. He is not trained and was formerly a saddler. His wages together with the cost of clothes, books, bands and dinner appear to be wholly wasted.' Despite Rawling's failings as a teacher he was a photographer of note and the scenes of Selby life are a lasting testament.

Introduction

The William Rawling Collection was donated to the Yorkshire Archaeological Society in 1960 by Doctor Morley, a direct descendant of the photographer, and is kept at Claremont in Leeds. William Rawling's son, titled William Rawling Morley, was a relative to Reg Morley who owned the tobacconists on Gowthorpe. Although William Rawling died in 1897, later photographs have been added to the collection to make this one of the most comprehensive and detailed of a Yorkshire town at the height of the Victorian and Edwardian era. Rawling must have been a familiar sight around the town, setting up his tripod and peering up at the light as the bustle of the market continued around him. His pictures are the essence of detail: the clothes, the workplace, the expressions on faces have all been captured by Rawling's lens. His work (supplemented with a few later photographs and cuttings) is presented here in its entirety for the first time showing fascinating scenes of the town and the surrounding area. Anyone with an interest in Selby will enjoy this nostalgic trip through the past.

Selby has its roots back in Saxon times. Observations made by Canon Raine and Doctor Gibson in the nineteenth century on the unearthing of an ancient burial ground confirm a Saxon connection. Fourteen coffins were found on Church Hill in a shallow burial ground similar to Saxon sites in Northumberland. Few personal possessions were found, suggesting that Selby was not a permanent settlement but a transitory camp for hunters and fishermen. A Viking settlement must also have resided in the area as many street names suggest: Mickle-gate (Great Way); Finkle Street (a corruption of the Viking 'vincle' meaning bend). The origin of the town's name (a contentious issue in itself) is probably derived from the fusion of the Saxon 'Sell' and the Viking 'Byr' meaning home or village.

The nucleus of the town grew around the Abbey established by Benedict of Auxerre and Viscount Hugh, the Sheriff of York, aided by grants of land in Selby, Flaxley, Rawcliffe, Brayton and Whitgift and the exclusive rights to grind corn, tax the sale of cattle and a certain legal jurisdiction. A cluster of cottages, inns, smithies and a tythe barn under Abbey control would have emerged, forming the roots of the present town.

Today Selby is a vibrant market town fighting to come to terms with a new economic era. The residents and ancestors at the turn of the century showed a confidence in the future, an unswerving faith in the monarchy and country and a belief in civic duty. The economic tide may have ebbed and flowed over a hundred years but contemporary Selebians still demonstrate a pride in their town and strong determination to succeed.

Acknowledgements

I am indebted to Richard Moody, who has allowed me access to his extensive research on the town. His weekly column in the *Selby Times* is a tribute to him and is enjoyed by so many.

My gratitude must also be extended to Mr Roger Philpot and Miss C.M.A. Baker for their information, and to the friendly staff of Selby Library.

Thanks go to Susan Leadbeater at the Yorkshire Archaeological Society for her help and patience.

This book is dedicated to Sue, Tim, Joe, Sam and Ashley

One

Selby Town and People

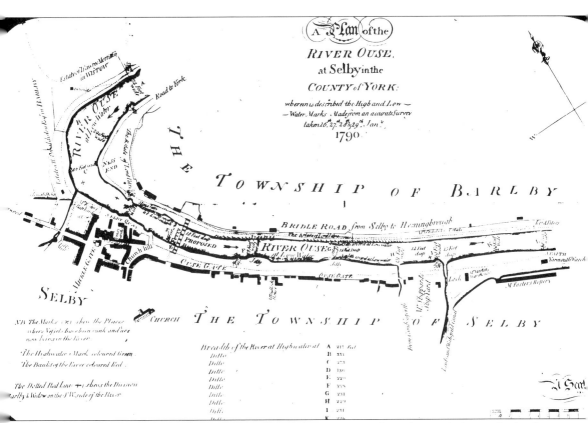

This map dated 1790 shows the water marks of the Ouse over three days and also marks (with an X) where vessels, obviously not having access to this map, have sunk.

An old etching looking down the Market Place. In view are the Abbey, cross and the stocks.

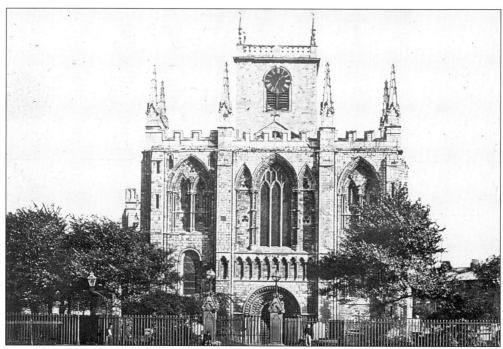

The Western Entrance to the Abbey from the Market Place *c.* 1890. The Western Towers were added during the 1930s.

Monday afternoon at the market. Sitting on the steps of the cross with one's thoughts (or an ice-cream) is a Selby tradition that has definitely not been lost during time. The cross, which is in Gothic style, was erected by 1790 and officially inaugurated by Robert Edward Petre, the 10th Baron and Lord of Londesborough.

Ed Gray's 'Cash Drug Store' on Market Day *c.* 1895. On sale were drugs of dubious medicinal origin such as pills, roots and herbs, and various parts of unknown species. In the days before the uniform use of antibiotics the competition to produce a cure for all manner of ailments was fierce: Selby Drug Stores at 6 Gowthorpe Street (under the ownership of Mr Brigham) sold 'Clarke's Blood Mixture' which claimed to cure scrofula, scurvy, eczema, ulcers, glandular

swellings, pimples and sores. This amazing liquid removed 'the cause from the blood' and was priced at 2s 9d a bottle. Another panacea was George Brown's Tamarind Glycerine and Blackcurrant Linctus which would cure coughs, hoarseness, bronchitis, asthma, influenza, and consumption – it was more reasonably priced at 1s 5d.

A Sunday Service at the Market Place *c.* 1906. After the Great Fire at the Abbey many such services were held outdoors – they proved to be especially popular. Outdoor services were also held during the Great War.

In 1900 Selebians celebrated the Relief of Mafeking by placing an effigy of the hated figure of General Kruger upon the Market Cross. Mafeking was a small South African town besieged by the Boers and its relief, at a time when the war had been going badly, was greeted with a national jubilation. The British contingent led by Baden-Powell held out for 215 days and the event was seen as a turning point in the fortunes of the war. General Kruger had refused equal rights to non-Boers – an action which had led to the Second Boer War. He became a form of 'bogeyman' to the British public (fuelled by regular vilifications in the national press) in the mould of a Hussein or Gaddaffi.

The bunting was out, flags fluttered and civic leaders thoroughly scrubbed when the Prince of Wales (later to become King Edward VII) visited the town on 21 November 1877. A special pagoda or 'arch' was constructed by Waters and Woodhouse of Scarborough at the cost of £450; obviously no local builder was deemed suitable to make such an auspicious temple of obsequiousness. The arch was draped in red, white and blue and decorated with a variety of flowers. The idea of inviting the Prince and demonstrating Selby's unstinting loyalty to the Crown, had been mooted a month earlier by William Liversidge who had found out that the Prince was to be guest of Lord Londesborough at a weekend shoot. The proposal to send an invitation was accepted by everyone at a special committee except Canon Harper. A true subversive malcontent Harper declared that the best way for Selebians to show their loyalty was 'to allow the Prince to enjoy his recreation without interruption'. However, the Canon's amendment to 'leave the Prince be' was rejected.

The Prince arrived in Selby to a downpour which carried on through the civic proceedings but did little to dampen enthusiasm as the streets were filled with people. The Prince thanked William Liversidge for his effusive welcome and left for his weekend shoot. Somewhat perversely the Selby Times reported that the Prince's party bagged 618 pheasants, 140 partridge and 186 hares.

A formal gathering, possibly for a Sunday Service, outside the Londesborough Hotel *c.* 1890. The Hotel was originally called 'The George' but its present title is derived from Selby's connection to Lord Londesborough, the Lord of the Manor.

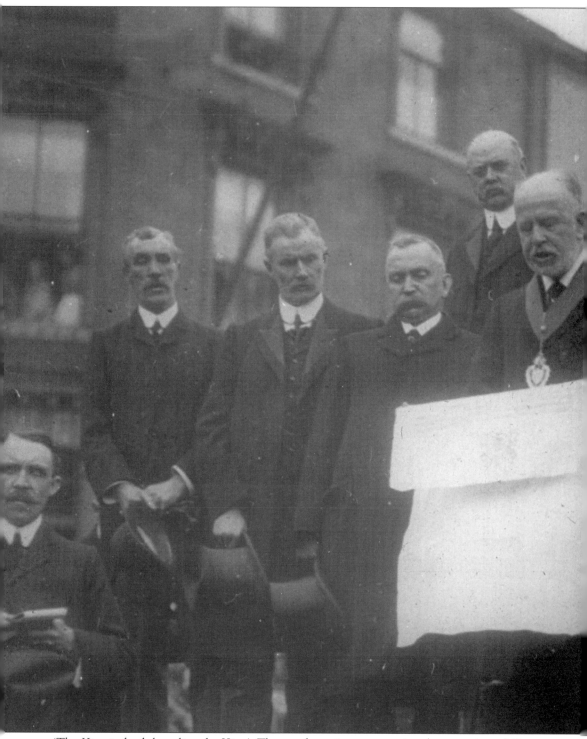

'The King is dead; long live the King'. The proclamation announcing the accession of George V to the throne was read from the Market Cross on 10 May 1910. The previous monarch,

Edward VII, had visited the town as the Prince of Wales in 1877 and the *Selby Times* reported 'great sadness' at his passing. Mr Mark Scott is pictured reading the proclamation.

The posting of Lord Kitchener's appeal for volunteers on the Market Cross 1914. The enthusiasm for the war at this stage was still strong: news of the horrors from Flanders filtered slowly through to the public's conscience. The Recruitment Office, headed by Mr W.H. Latimer, was at 4 Park Street. Selby's young responded to the call to arms – a testament borne out by the many names displayed within the Abbey.

Market Day at Selby, *c.* 1890. The fertile area around the Ouse has always encouraged agriculture and Selby became the natural focus for the market.

A modern view of the steps, still a popular resting place for tired legs.

Jack Stevens' grocery stall at Selby Market, *c.* 1890. Mr Stevens' selling cry is a famous part of Selby History. 'Civil oranges, oranges from civil' would resound around the Market Place. ('Civil' otherwise being a city in Spain called Seville).

The Albert Hotel on Micklegate *c.* 1890. This Elizabethan property was formerly the Curriers Arms but at this time was occupied by Beasley's Fruit and Veg and the Boot Repairing Depot. It was demolished about 1913 to make way for the General Post Office.

In 1963 the old General Post Office was demolished and replaced with the hideous box pictured here. Lacking any charm or beauty the present incumbent is a sad example of the 1960s functionalism – Selby deserved better.

Ambrose Chambers as a young man in the 1860s. Chambers came from a notable Selby family and his name appears upon many local committees at the turn of the century. He was a member of the School Board for many years but retired in 1911. He was a butcher by trade and ran a shop at 35 Micklegate.

A rare view across the park encapsulating the full length of the Abbey's southern side c.1870. Such a view would only be possible today through an extensive de-forestation of the park and the removal of the heavy goods vehicles thundering past.

A group at
Micklegate,
c. 1880.

A modern view to the Abbey from Micklegate looking between The Griffin and the Post Office.

Recent developments in the town have removed many of the old 'Yards' rendering identification problematic. A Yard was an enclosed piece of land containing workshops, homes and a larger house owned by a person who maintained all the properties: the Yards would usually be named after these prominent individuals, hence Hope's Yard and Addinal's Yard. After the publication of this photograph in the *Selby Times* several suggestions have emerged for its whereabouts, including the back of the Nelson Inn on Ousegate.

A view down Church Avenue toward Church Lane *c.* 1960. Originally the entrance to Church Lane was crossed by four 'bollards' but two were removed just after the war to aid access.

SELBY, 9th November, 1831.

Cholera Morbus.

RULES AND REGULATIONS

To be observed by the Inhabitants of SELBY and Neighbourhood to prevent and relieve the dreadful Disease called *Cholera Morbus* (as ordered by the Secretary of State, Magistrates, and Board of Health) and to which they are particularly desired to attend.

(As submitted by Mr. J. Fothergill, and approved by the Committee.)

KEEP your houses and premises clean.

Open your windows and doors frequently, and admit fresh air.

Dress out and cleanse all drains, channels, and other places, and take away all sorts of manure, filth, dirt, or any other material which is likely to cause infection.

Whitewash your houses occasionally with quick lime, from the cellar to the garret.

If there be the *least* appearance of the disease, immediately inform the Medical Practitioners, the Board of Health, or the Churchwardens and Overseers.

Burn all decayed articles belonging to your house, such as rags, cordages, old papers, old clothes, old hangings, &c. which are not of any value or use.

Where it is possible, cleanse and wash out your drains and privies with water.

Place in your houses, according to their size, one or more teacups or other vessel, filled with salt-petre or common salt, upon which pour small quantities of oil of vitriol and water, one of the former to two of the latter, and frequently stir with a piece of wood or a quill.

Keep your persons clean, and as often as you are able put on clean linen.

Live with great temperance, particularly avoiding the use of Spirituous Liquors, as the great mischief and the most deaths have been caused by such practices.

Keep within doors, or under cover, during the evening as much as possible, as exposure to the night dew might assist in causing the complaint.

Sprinkle hot vinegar in your rooms frequently.

Clothe the surface of your bodies as well as you are able, more especially by flannel wore next the skin.

Smoke tobacco.

The Chloride of Lime, where it can be purchased, might be used with advantage in sprinkling about the houses, or washing any article of furniture with.

Along with the above precautionary measures, all persons are desired to unite cordially in offering up their Prayers, generally and severally to Almighty God that he may be pleased to avert from this land of Great Britain so dreadful a calamity.

The above measures and precautionary means are particularly advised and desired to be effected, by persons living in confined streets and yards, or where the population is crowded, as places of that kind have suffered the most.

All public officers such as surveyors of highways, juries, overseers, churchwardens, scavengers, &c. are ordered and desired to cause all filth, manure, and other public nuisance to be removed, and to employ the unemployed poor in cleansing, scouring, &c. all drains, sewers, streets, lanes, channels, &c. in a frequent and effectual manner.

S. W. WAUD,
CHAIRMAN.

J. Muncaster, Minister.

CHURCHWARDENS.
Daniel Macgregor
William Hawdon
John Bradley
James Banks

OVERSEERS.
David Hick
John Green
Jonathan Briggs
John Lamb

SURGEONS.
J. Fothergill, M. R. C. S.
J. Fothergill, Jun. M. R. C. S.
R. Addinell
J. Burkitt, M. R. C. S. &c.
A. Graham

A poster from 1831 describing, for the benefit of Selby citizens, ways to avoid cholera. This year saw the first large scale outbreaks throughout Western Europe and at first links were made with the plague. The disease is an acute infection of the small intestine by the bacterium *Vibrio cholerae* which causes vomiting and diarrhoea. It breeds in water contaminated by faeces and if consumed results in rapid dehydration. It came to Europe from the Far East along the ancient trading routes and found an ideal breeding ground in the unhygenic conditions of Britain's newly industrialised cities. The poster has several recommendations including smoking, keeping under cover at night, offering prayers and discouraging the use of alcohol.

CHOLERA BURIAL GROUND

IN THE CHOLERA EPIDEMIC OF 1848/1849 OVER ONE HUNDRED PEOPLE DIED IN THE SELBY AREA. THE WORST AFFLICTED STREETS WERE MILLGATE, MICKLEGATE, FINKLE STREET AND OUSEGATE. THE WORKHOUSE WAS ALSO BADLY AFFECTED. A RELIEF COMMITTEE VISITED EIGHT HUNDRED HOUSES AND SUPPLIED THREE HUNDRED AND FIFTY EIGHT FAMILIES WITH NECESSITIES.

THE OVERUSED PARISH GRAVEYARD AROUND THE ABBEY CHURCH, WHICH, AS NOW, WAS SURROUNDED BY THESE CAST IRON RAILINGS ERECTED IN 1828, WAS UNABLE TO ACCOMMODATE MANY OF THE VICTIMS OF THE EPIDEMIC WHO WERE THEREFORE INTERRED IN THE AREA IN FRONT OF THIS NOTICE.

AS A RESULT OF THE EPIDEMIC, WORKS WERE PUT IN HAND BOTH TO PROVIDE A PIPED WATER SUPPLY AND TO OVERHAUL COMPLETELY THE DECAYED DRAINAGE SYSTEM IN THE TOWN. THE PARISH GRAVEYARD WAS CLOSED AND THE CEMETERY ADJACENT TO THE BRAYTON ROAD WAS INAUGURATED IN 1868.

SELBY CIVIC SOCIETY 1994 SELBY DISTRICT COUNCIL

The plaque displayed on the Abbey railings describes the cholera epidemic which struck Selby in 1848 and 1849. Such were the numbers of dead (over one hundred) a 'convenient burial ground' was established at Abbey Place.

The Abbey Place burial ground.

A view down Church Lane c. 1885. On the left is 'Daddy' Coulan.

A modern view of Church Lane. The Abbey is now partly obscured by the trees but the houses on the right side have altered only in the transfer of the lamp from across the Lane.

The Abbey Tythe Barn c. 1896. The barn would have been established by the monks of the Abbey Church to store the grain presented by the local population as part of their Medieval dues.

In 1896 the Tythe Barn began to be demolished – a process that was well photographed. Pictured among the ruins is Joseph Morley, possibly a relative of William Rawling.

Local children pose at the demolition site *c.* 1896. As for all children a site of destruction is always far more interesting than one of construction.

The final stages of the process *c.* 1896.

A view across Selby Bowling Green to the site of the Barn which stretched from the Safeway Superstore to the Infants School.

The Civic Society plaque gives a 'potted' history of the Tythe Barn and resides in the walls of the new shopping arcade.

The old Blue Bell Inn which stood on Ousegate.

The site of the Blue Bell Inn is today owned by the General Freight Company situated next door to the Nelson public house. At the turn of the century Ousegate was the major thoroughfare in Selby but the street at present is a faded, quiet relic of its past.

Canon and Mrs Harper in the vicarage garden *c.* 1880. Canon Harper gave robust religious lessons at the Abbey School. Each morning he would declare to his nervous collection of pupils: 'And will you work this morning well?' The solemn reply would always be 'our very best we'll do'. The Canon kept a large selection of keys on a leather bootlace around his waist – any pupil stepping out of line would receive the full weight of these upon a chosen limb.

After his death the local newspaper received an envelope of his own addressing in which was contained a handwritten obituary: 'The influence of Canon Harper's noble life will long survive him and preach a powerful sermon to those who live after him.'

A modern view of the 'old' Vicarage.

A Victorian scene at the back of a Selby House *c.* 1890.

Selebians pose for Rawling's camera *c.* 1890.

Bill Simpson was a Selby grocer and owned the site at 22/24 Gowthorpe *c.* 1885. We must assume that he was very proud of this large plant which is portrayed with him in this Rawling photograph.

Nos 24/26/28 Gowthorpe is still a grocers. W.H. Whisker & Sons occupies three sites on the street.

Benjamin Connell in military uniform *c*. 1885. Connell came from a locally famous Selby family that had interests in the shipping business. The company launched its last ship in the 1920s and did contract work during the 1930s and '40s, before turning its attention to yachts. It finally closed in 1958. Ben Connell's address in *Slater's Yorkshire Directory* is listed as 'The George Hotel' (formerly the Petre Arms, it eventually became the Londesborough). Connell was born in 1840 and was the leaseholder of the George; he died on 2 March 1897. The Connell family also for many years had possession of 'The Serpent' (see page 94) and were the driving force behind Selby Rugby Football Club.

SELBY.

To be SOLD by AUCTION,

At the GEORGE INN in SELBY,

On MONDAY the 9th Day of MAY next, at Four o'Clock in the Afternoon, (unlefs difpofed of in the mean-time by Private Contract, of which Notice will be given) fubject to fuch Conditions of Sale as fhall be then and there produced,

A Large, fubftantial, and commodious FREEHOLD DWELLING-HOUSE, fituate near the North-Eaft End of MICKLEGATE, in SELBY aforefaid, wherein Mrs. Smith now dwells, with a good Yard and fpacious Gardens behind the fame, planted with choice Fruit Trees, and the Common-Right and other Conveniences and Appurtenances thereunto adjoining or belonging.

Alfo a Three-Stand STABLE adjoining the Premifes, which might at a moderate Expence be converted into a Warehoufe, and occupied either with or feparate from the Houfe.

The Purchafer may have Poffeffion of the Houfe and Premifes on the 12th of May next.

For further Particulars apply at the Office of Mr. E..., Attorney, in Selby aforefaid.

SELBY, 20th APRIL, 1796.

An auction poster for the George Inn in 1796.

A rather elaborate advert for Reg Morley's Tobacco Shop at 73 Gowthorpe c. 1955. Reg Morley was related to William Rawling.

The present owner of 73 Gowthorpe is Shaw's Pastimes, an amusement arcade.

Colonel G.R. Lane-Fox (on the left) was the Conservative Member of Parliament for Selby from 1906 to 1931 when he was then elevated to the peerage. He is pictured here with Mr Bantoft.

Lane-Fox M.P. at the hunt. In the 110 years of the Selby Constituency only four members (all Conservatives) have been returned to Westminster. However in 1905 a Liberal candidate, Mr Andrew, was voted in at a by-election but he failed to take his seat in Parliament as a snap General Election saw Lane-Fox returned. The use of babies and children to elicit sympathy during campaigning was not unusual even in Edwardian times: Lane-Fox paraded his two young daughters around the streets of Selby during an election under the banner 'please vote for daddy'.

Martin Pearson, *c.* 1860. Pearson, a successful Selby solicitor, formed a partnership with a Mr Howden. He chaired the committee formed after the 1848-49 cholera epidemic to establish a clean and safe water supply.

The partnership used decorated envelopes designed from a pattern drawn in 1447.

Mr Charles Weddall lived at West Bank Hall, Carlton and was a local Selby magistrate. His older brother, Thomas Motley Weddall, became a partner in the local solicitor's firm in 1842 after the retirement of Edward Parker. By 1888 the firm was known as Weddall, Parker and Parker but after Thomas's death in 1891 the family moved to Leeds. The Weddall name was removed in 1912. Today the firm of Parker, March, Charlton and Eastman resides on the corner of St James Street and Abbey Yard.

Mr Richardson was a Selby draper and long standing member of the local school board.

The Hutchinson Family *c.* 1850. This rare and very old picture shows Jonathan Hutchinson upon the knee of his Grandfather while his father holds a portrait of his Great Grandfather. Sir Johnathan Hutchinson became an eminent pathologist and founded the Haslemere Educational Museum in West Sussex. His creation of the Selby Museum at the Museum Hall in 1900 was accompanied by the donation of many exhibits including a stuffed Bengal tiger and an Egyptian mummy. However interest in the museum eventually waned and the exhibits were distributed to unknown sources. The main hall was then used for concerts, bazaars, wedding receptions, and from 1920 onwards regular Monday evening dances were held.

A collection of torture instruments that were displayed at the Selby Museum c. 1902. Amongst the macabre and gruesome implements were a display of flails, knives, clubs and a set of sugar loaf tongs. The flail or lash had been the symbol of discipline within the prison service (and the military) for over two centuries: it consisted of knotted strips of leather hardened by soaking in water. The victims of flagellation would be left with a criss-cross of scars upon their backs.

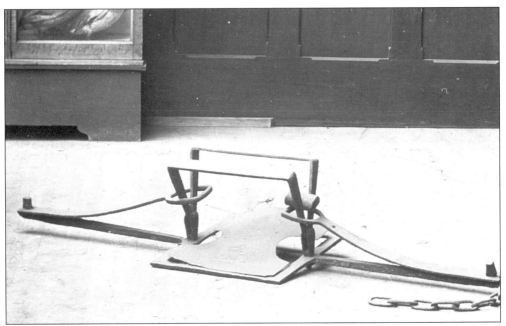

A nasty and potentially lethal man-trap on display at Selby Museum c. 1902. Such devices, still in use on many estates throughout the Victorian era, were the bane of poachers' lives and could lead to amputation and sometimes death.

TEN GUINEAS REWARD.

WHEREAS, on the Morning of SUNDAY, the 19th. instant, between the Hours of One and Three o'Clock,

FIVE POACHERS,

ARMED WITH BLUDGEONS,

DOGS of the LURCHER Kind, and One a Sort of CUR,

WERE FOUND TRESPASSING ON THE GROUNDS OF THE

Hon. E. PETRE, at BRAYTON, near Selby,

And made a violent Attack on several of the Watchers, Three of whom were much cut and wounded about the head. The Poachers are supposed to be much wounded, and one of them shot in the legs.

One Poacher, a Little Man, had on a Short Blue-striped Smock,—another, a Tall Man, described as being from 5 ft. 10 to 11 in. high, had on a Dark Velveteen Jacket, the Front of which was burnt in the Affray. It is supposed that the Poachers are all more or less hurt in their Persons. After the Affray, the Poachers went in the direction of Gateforth.

Whoever will give such Information to Mr. D. HICK, Constable of SELBY, as will lead to the Conviction of the Offenders, will be paid a Reward of TEN GUINEAS.

October 19th. 1841

A reward of ten guineas posted in Brayton and Selby for the capture of poachers. Despite the risks of capture and prosecution 'poaching' was for many a way of life made necessary in order to supplement a meagre diet.

The Victorian taste for the strange and macabre was always evident – in the days before television, entertainment was usually live and transient. The cost of a shilling to see a man twenty-six inches high would have been prohibitive for many Selebians.

GENERAL TOM THUMB.

The American Man in Miniature!!

Under the Patronage of HER MAJESTY THE QUEEN, the Queen Dowager, the KING AND QUEEN OF THE BELGIANS, H. R. H. Prince Albert, H. R. H. the Duchess of Kent, Dukes of Cambridge, Wellington, Devonshire, Buckingham, &c., and visited in London by

300,000 Persons in four months.

The Inhabitants of Selby are respectfully informed that the

LITTLE GENERAL

Will hold his public Levees

AT THE

PUBLIC ROOM,
SELBY,

On Tuesday, Oct. 29th.
FOR ONE DAY ONLY.

General Tom Thumb

Is smaller than any Infant that ever walked alone, **being 25 inches high** and **weighing only 15 Pounds.**

He is of the most symmetrical proportions, is lively, intelligent, and graceful in his manners—he will relate his history—represent NAPOLEON in full MILITARY COSTUME—delineate the GRECIAN STATUES—give a variety of SONGS and DANCES, &c., and will also appear in his magnificent Court Dress, which he had the honour of wearing three times before Her Majesty.

The beautiful presents from Her Majesty, the Queen Dowager, the Duke of Devonshire, &c., may be seen.

Hours of Exhibition from 11 to 1, 3 to 5, and from 7 to 9 Admission, (regardless of age) **One Shilling.**

The General's Miniature Equipage will arrive early on Tuesday from Hull per Railway.

T. Hutchinson, Printer, &c., Church-yard, Selby.

A ticket for a public breakfast with Hon. Mrs Petre. The Petre family were the Lords to the ancient manor around Selby.

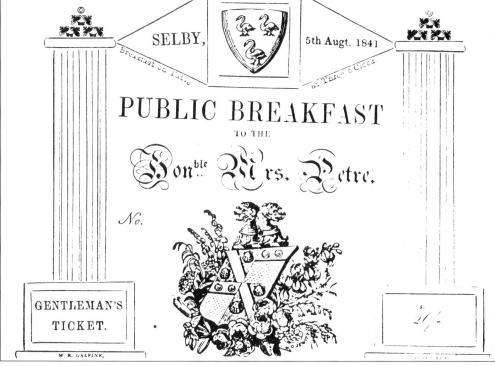

SELBY,   5th Augt. 1841

Breakfast on Table   at Three o'Clock

PUBLIC BREAKFAST

TO THE

Honble Mrs. Petre.

No.

GENTLEMAN'S TICKET.

W. R. GALPINE,

The Wesleyan Chapel in James Street *c.* 1870.

Selby Quaker Chapel on Gowthorpe, *c.* 1880. The site of this chapel is now occupied by Radio Rentals but a burial ground remains at the back. The Quaker headstones were brought to Gowthorpe site from the Summercroft burial site.

The Revd Andrew Burns was the Catholic priest at the Church on Gowthorpe from 1872 to 1902.

A modern view of the present Catholic Church – the original Church stood at the corner of Brook Street and Gowthorpe but was replaced in 1856.

Captain Henry Liversidge in full Scottish dress *c.* 1870.

The three Liversidge Brothers: Henry, William and Thomas c. 1900. The Liversidge Brothers played an extensive part in the history of Selby as employers and civic patrons. They owned several businesses including an agricultural merchants on Ousegate and had various engineering and shipbuilding interests. William, a local magistrate, paid for the restoration of the famous East window in the Abbey in 1889 (and the subsequent replacement after the 1906 fire). Thomas and Henry were representatives upon many notable local committees. William lived at Millgate House; Thomas at Brooklands and Henry in Sherburn.

This group of ladies were representatives of Selby Women's Christian Temperance Society which gathered to listen to services on Christian values. One such speech was conducted by a Miss Capper of Leeds on the subject of 'The Weaver's Shuttle'.

William Littlewood on his twenty-first birthday. A plaque to a William Littlewood resides in the Abbey. A William Littlewood Ridge was also the schoolmaster at the Wesleyan Day School before the turn of the century and prepared the written history of Wesleyans in Selby. Which of these Selebians was photographed by Rawling remains unsolved.

Pupils and Miss Tiplady outside the school house *c.* 1870.

Dr Kenney with his family and Dr Somers. Dr Maurice Aloysius Kenny was for many years the Medical Officer to Selby Workhouse and his surgery is listed as being 7, The Crescent. He received his training at Edinburgh University and practised in Selby throughout his career.

Number Seven, The Crescent, the site of Dr Kenney's surgery, is to the right of the National Westminster Bank and is today a hairdresser's.

This group of prominent Wesleyans appear to have their heads superimposed upon different bodies – an intriguing puzzle. Left to right, top row: Mr Twist, Mr Morley, Mr Turner, Mr Stables, Mr Swain, Mr Banks. Third row: Mr Mark Stables, Mr J. Dunn, Mr J. Rimmington, Mr Richardson, Mr Moss, Mr Gillian, Mr Sherwood. Second row: Mr Foster, Minister, Minister, Mr Haigh, Mr Morrell. Front row: Mr R. Taylor, Mr W. Glew, Minister, Mr Brooksbank, Mr Lowther, Mr Bairstow.

Rifle volunteers of the 1st West Riding L Company *c.* 1900. Their headquarters at this time were at the Drill Hall in Brook Street and were led by Major Tom Gibson Hawdon; Lieutenant J.G.P. Parker Toulson and Drill Instructor George Hancock.

Enlisted members of the 1st Battalion West Yorkshire Regiment outside the General Post Office in Micklegate c. 1914. Throughout the war the *Selby Times* kept in touch with 'our lads'. Lance Corporal R. Dawson of Olympia Cottages, Barlby Road, was asked: 'Are the Germans bad fellows?' His reply stated: 'Oh, no, they are not bad fellows, and they are very pleased to get into our hands and be taken prisoner.' Mrs Long of Olympia Cottages perhaps felt a little less kindly to the Germans; she had five sons serving, one of whom is listed upon the Abbey Memorial Plaque.

Troops at drill, *c.* 1914. During the four years of the War the British Empire was to lose over 900,000 lives. Such sweeping destruction of a generation created such a population imbalance that for several years many women remained unmarried.

Wash and brush-up, *c.* 1914.

PEACE REJOICINGS

SELBY!

THE INHABITANTS OF SELBY, ARE HEREBY INFORMED THAT

ON THURSDAY, THE 29th DAY OF MAY, 1856.

PUBLIC REJOICINGS

On account of the Definitive Treaty of Peace and Friendship, now happily concluded between Her MAJESTY the QUEEN and Her ALLIES, and His Imperial Majesty the EMPEROR of all the RUSSIAS, will take place in the following order:

1. The above day will be observed as *A GENERAL HOLIDAY*, and will be ushered in by the *Ringing of Bells* and the *Firing of Cannon*, which will be continued at intervals during the day.

2. *At Ten o'clock in the Forenoon*, the Committee and such other Inhabitants as desire to do so, will meet at the TOWN-HALL, and after assembling there will proceed to the MARKET-CROSS, where THE QUEENS PROCLAMATION will be publicly read, followed by DISCHARGES OF CANNON, after which a PROCESSION will be formed to march round the Town.

3. *At One o'clock at Noon*, the WORKING-MEN of SELBY, will be entertained at DINNER in a spacious Marquee, erected in the Market-place.

4. *At Three o'clock in the Afternoon*, the CHILDREN of the Working-Classes between the Ages of 7 and 16 years, will take TEA in the Marquee.

5. *At Five o'clock, in the Evening*, the WIVES and DAUGHTERS of the Working-Men, and YOUNG WOMEN of 16 years of Age and upwards, will sit down to TEA together in the same place.

6. *At Eight o'clock in the Evening*, there will be A GRAND DISPLAY of FIRE WORKS, FIRING of ROCKETS, BLUE LIGHTS, &c., in the Bowling Green.

7. The NAVAL BAND of the Right Honourable Lord LONDESBOROUGH, (by permission of his Lordship,) and other Bands, will be present on the occasion and perform at intervals throughout the day.

GENERAL REGULATIONS.

It is requested that all persons assisting, or taking part in the proceedings of the day, will endeavour to promote their success and the harmony of the ceremony to the utmost, by observing the strictest decorum and propriety of conduct in every respect.

The DINNER and TEAS will be under the immediate superintendence of the Committee of Management, the Members of which will be distinguished by a White Rosette on the left breast, and the Officers by a White Riband at the Button-hole.

GOD save the QUEEN?

BY ORDER.

JAMES AUDUS, Chairman.

SELBY, MAY 16th, 1856.

N.B. A PUBLIC DINNER at the LONDESBOROUGH ARMS, at Seven o'clock in the Evening, Tickets 10s 6d each to be had at the Bar.

A poster declaring the end to the Crimean War c. 1856.

The Selby
Rifle Band
pose for the
camera in the
grounds of
Carlton
Towers
c. 1888.

A drawing of Don Juan the racehorse photographed by William Rawling.

Death of Don Juan.

——oo——

(From the Yorkshireman of June 19, 1841.)

——◦oo——

DON JUAN.—We are sorry to inform our sporting friends, as well as breeders and others, that the celebrated stallion Don Juan, the property of Edward Wormald, Esq , of Cawood Castle, near Selby, died at Thorne on the 3rd inst., aged 25 years. He was bred by his Majesty George the Fourth, at Hampton Court, and was own brother to Gustavus (winner of the Epsom Derby in 1821), got by Election, out of Lady Grey, own sister to Viscount, by Stamford , grandam by Bourdeaux ; great grandam by Prophet, out of Saltrem's dam. Don Juan has long distinguished himself as one of the first sires of superior hunters, &c., in the kingdom ; and his worth and excellence having invoked the muse to perpetuate his fame, we enjoin his epitaph :—

In memory of that celebrated thorough-bred Stallion
DON JUAN,
own brother, to Gustavus, by Election,
out of Lady Grey, by Stamford ;
bred by his Majesty George the Fourth, when Prince Regent,
and purchased by Edward Wormald, Esq.,
of Cawood Castle, near Selby,
in whose possession he died at Thorne,
June 3rd, 1841.

" Stop, reader stop, let nature claim a tear,
A friend of mine, " Don Juan," lies buried here ;
Of royal blood he won himself a name,
Which ne'er will die in annals of good fame ;
Many's the year he gave bold reynard chase,
And ne'er was found defaulter in his race ;
In good old age his withers were unwrung,
'Till that grim tyrant, death, his heart unstrung ;
Yet many of his race he's left behind,
That prove he was superior to his kind.
In honour, then, unto his well-earn'd fame,
And gratefully to perpetuate his name,
I pay this tribute o'er his sodden grave,
And thus pronounce him bravest of the brave."

Thorne, June 3rd, 1841.   **W. W.**

Don Juan's obituary 1841.

George Lowther relaxes in the garden of his house on St James Terrace *c.* 1880. Lowther was the town's Registrar for many years and a leading Estate Agent. His name appears on more local documents in this period than any other Selebian. He gave a series of lectures on the history of Selby at the Public Rooms; he died in 1894.

Lowther's home at 8 St James Terrace.

Thomas Hardisty was a cabinet maker and joiner who lived on Audus Street. His son Richard continued in the business and worked with Elwell of Beverley and was responsible for carving many of the wooden decorations after the Abbey Fire of 1906.

William Farley c. 1880. Farley was a prominent journalist with the *Selby Times* and his brother Robert sold pottery and china at a shop in the Market Place.

In the back streets of Selby *c.* 1880.

Thomas Leaper, a prominent
Selebian, *c.* 1875.

Dr J. Fothergill
junior, *c.* 1880. Drs
Fothergill (father
and son) were the
local medical
officers in Selby.
Both of their
names appear on
Cholera Morbus
poster of 1881 (see
page 30).

Two

Transportation

For six years Selby was at the hub of Yorkshire's communications. The Leeds–Selby line, completed in 1834, terminated in Selby and a transfer was then made to waiting boats. The extension of the railway to Hull in 1840 immediately killed this infant industry. These fares were printed in the *Yorkshire Weekly Post* on 15 May 1915.

The Grand opening of the Cawood, Wistow and Selby Railway Line, February 1898. The original Leeds to Selby Line had been completed by 1834 but attempts to link Selby to the villages had failed. The *Selby Times* had reported that local farmers had objected to the project on the grounds that it 'would destroy the need for horses'. Eventually the financial backing was secured and the connection was made before the turn of the century. The Lord Mayor of York,

Alderman Gray, officially opened the line but as so often happens on such civic occasions the weather deemed to play a part: the Mayor's speech was drowned out by a gale while invited guests fought to hold onto their hats and cloaks. Captain Liversidge also spoke at the ceremony and declared that the new line would not be known as a 'light' railway as that would be 'undignified'; obviously the Cawood to Selby line was thought to require a certain 'gravitas'.

A drawing of the view across the Ouse to the Abbey *c.* 1750.

The Lock Keeper's House and Lazy Cut on the Selby Canal *c.* 1880.

The old Bascule Railway Bridge across the Ouse was built in 1840 and demolished in 1891.

Boats on the Ouse c. 1900. In the background the old Blue Bell Inn is still visible on Ousegate.

CHEAP & EXPEDITIOUS CONVEYANCE,

DAILY, BY THE

CALEDONIA & WATERLOO

STEAM PACKETS,

FROM HULL TO SELBY.

GOODS by these Packets, are forwarded from Selby, every day, by Widow Welsh & Son's Fly Waggons, to

LEEDS,	MANCHESTER, and
BRADFORD,	LIVERPOOL;
HALIFAX,	ALSO TO
ROCHDALE,	DEWSBURY, and
OLDHAM,	HUDDERSFIELD.

The CALEDONIA and WATERLOO STEAM PACKET COMPANY return their sincere thanks to their Friends and the Public, for the liberal support they have received, and hope, by punctuality and dispatch, to merit a continuance of the same. They beg to inform them that they have appointed

Mr. THOMAS ELLIS,

4. KINGSTON-COURT, BLANKET-ROW, NEW DOCK WALLS, their AGENT; who will give every information required. WAREHOUSE for GOODS, at Mr. HOLMES's, GOLDEN CUP, HUMBER-STREET.

The WATERLOO having been recently furnished with a new Engine, Boiler, &c. of very superior power, is now the most complete Packet on the River for safety and dispatch.

☞ COACHES for LEEDS, YORK, and WAKEFIELD Wait the arrival of the above Packets at Selby.

Hull, Sept. 21st. 1820.

RULES

AND

REGULATIONS

TO BE

Observed by the Proprietors

OF THE

WATERLOO STEAM PACKET,

AND BY

Their Treasurer, Committee, and other Persons intrusted therein.

SELBY:

PRINTED AT THE OFFICE OF W. BOOTH.

Top, left: An advertisement for the Caledonian and Waterloo Steam Packet. Top, right: Rules and Regulations on the Steam Packet.

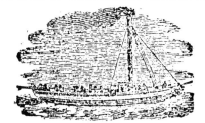

WATERLOO STEAM PACKET.

TO BE SOLD BY AUCTION,

At the House of Mr. Robert Addinell, the New Inn, in Selby, on Friday, the 17th day of August, 1821, at Four o'clock in the afternoon,

(Subject to the Conditions then to be produced,)

THE substantial Steam Packet called "The WATERLOO," which sails between SELBY and HULL; fitted up not only with every requisite for the comfort and accommodation of a very great number of Passengers, but also calculated to take Bale Goods, &c.; with the Engine, Engine Work (nearly new), Boat, Stores and Appurtenances thereto belonging.

Further Particulars may be had at Mr. PARKER's Office in Selby.

The business was auctioned by Edward Parker's Office in 1821.

The *Joanna* was one of the most popular steam packets to ply the route between Selby and Hull. The packets' heyday ran from 1780 to the 1830s. The fare for the *Joanna* was 2 shillings; an extra 6d for men and 4d for women was charged if meals were served.

The Joanna,

R.. ...TATE, MASTER,

WILL sail m..SE... ..s HULL every Monday, and take in Goods and Passengers for all Places adjoining the Rivers OUSE and HUMBER; the faid Veffel will also sail from HULL to SELBY every Thursday, if Wind and Weather permit, and will take in Goods and Paffengers for SELBY, and all Places adjoining thereto.

Passengers from Selby to Hull to pay two fhillings, and find themselves, but if the Vessel find them Victuals, then, Men to pay Sixpence, and Women Fourpence for each Meal.

Further Particulars may be had of Captain Thorn... at the Sign of the Duke of Clarence, South End, HULL, or at Mr. Barton's New Inn, SELBY, from which Place a Stage Waggon goes to LEEDS every Monday and returns on Tuefdays; Orders are alfo taken at Richard Tate's Houfe Broad Street, SELBY,

Thofe Perfons who pleafe to favour the faid Richard Tate with their Goods may depend upon having them forwarded with the quickeft Difpatch.

The Veffel is in good Repair and has excellent Accommodations for Paffengers.

Below, left: The 'Packet' owners, keen to establish further business, created a carriage service into Selby from various Yorkshire towns and cities.

Below, right: Sailing times from the Caledonia Steam Packet.

THE CALEDONIA YORK DILIGENCE.

THE PROPRIETORS of the CALEDONIA STEAM PACKET beg to inform their Friends and the Public, that they have established the above DILIGENCE, which runs every MONDAY, WEDNESDAY, and FRIDAY Mornings, from Mrs. CLAYTON's, ROBIN HOOD, Castlegate, York, to Selby; from which place Goods and Passengers are forwarded by the PACKET the same Evening to HULL. The YORK DILIGENCE waits the return of the PACKET on the following days from HULL to SELBY, when it immediately sets off for York.

Inside Fare for the Coach and the best Cabin from York to Hull, 9s.—Outside ditto and the Fore-Cabin from York to Hull, 6s. 6d.—Inside Fare from York to Selby, 4s. 6d.—Outside ditto, 3s. 6d.

The *Caledonia Steam Packet Company* hope their Friends and the Public will not attend to the Reports lately circulated, by their Opponents of the same day, as they can affure them of the CALEDONIA being the speediest Packet, with very handsome accommodations for Passengers, and where they will meet with every attention.

☞ For further Particulars, apply to Mr. CLOSE, manager at Hull; or Mr. SENIOR, London Tavern.

9, *New Dock Walls, Hull, 5th July*, 1819.

Caledonia Steam Packet,
FROM HULL TO SELBY.

THE CALEDONIA STEAM PACKET COMPANY, beg leave most respectfully to inform their Friends and the Public, that they have purchased that safe, elegant and commodious STEAM PACKET, the CALEDONIA which leaves Hull for Selby every Tuesday, Thursday, and Saturday, and returns from Selby, every Monday, Wednesday, and Friday Morning, at NINE o'clock, after the arrival of the LEEDS and WAKEFIELD COACHES.

As they have fitted up the Packet, in a most complete manner, for the Accommodation of Passengers, as well as for the secure conveyance of Bale Goods, &c. they take the liberty of soliciting the support of the public, who may rest assured that every thing will be done to render the Conveyance expeditious, comfortable, and convenient.

Fare to Selby—Best Cabin 6s. Second Cabin 4s.

Goods to and from Manchester, Halifax, Huddersfield, Bradford, Leeds, &c. &c. will be forwarded by this Conveyance with the utmost dispatch; if consigned to the following Persons:—

Widow WELSH and SONS, Ducer-street, Manchester.
  Ditto   Ditto   Canal Warehouse, Huddersfield.
  Ditto   Ditto   Bank-street, Leeds.
    JOSHUA FARRER, Market-place, Halifax.
    T. WARD, Bowling-Green, Bradford.

☞ For further Particulars and Information apply to Mr. CLOSE, No. 9, *New Dock Walls*; who is appointed Manager at Hull.

N. B. All Goods arriving by this Packet, will be delivered as addressed free of porterage.

A model of the Toll Bridge on display. Those with keen eyes will notice the model has many more supports than the full-scale version.

The *Water Lily* docked at
Lazy Cut *c.* 1890.

A long boat enters the lock at the meeting of the Ouse and Selby canal. The lock-keepers house
and Lazy Cut are just beyond this point.

Mr Beswick – Water Bailiff c. 1910.

A rare sight: ice floes on the Ouse near Selby c. 1897.

A working mill, c. 1900.

The old soke mill at
Selby was demolished
in 1886.

Children look at the *Water Lily* at Lazy Cut *c*. 1890. The expansion of Selby and her industries is intrinsically linked to the growth in trade throughout the West Riding and the need to secure a viable route to the sea. Rising tolls for trading vessels on the Aire and Calder rivers forced manufacturers to consider an alternative link. In 1774 William Jessop secured a Parliamentary Act connecting Aire to Ouse by canal. The five mile stretch from Haddlesey to Selby brought trade back to the area – in 1800 nearly 400,000 tons of goods passed through. In 1826 the Aire Calder Navigation Company built a new canal from Knottingley to Goole where new docks were constructed, bypassing Selby.

This ship appears to be on the canal *c.* 1890.

A bridge on the Selby Canal *c.* 1870.

BRAYTON TOLL GATE.

Brayton Toll Gate was constructed under the provisions of the Turnpike Acts which allowed the construction of new roads funded by the payment of tolls – a form of road building that may well be coming back into fashion. Despite the general upheaval caused by the transition (there was a riot in 1752) the Turnpikes proved extremely profitable. The toll taken at the Brayton Toll Gate was £1,565 in 1808 rising to £2,235 in 1834. What killed the Turnpike Roads was the arrival of the railway into Selby which removed much of the commercial business.

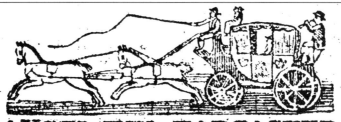

ANGEL INN, TADCASTER.

MATTHEW KIDD avails himself of this opportunity, to inform the Public, that a Coach Runs daily from HARROGATE and KNARESBRO', &c. by way of Wetherby and Tadcaster, every Morning (Sundays excepted), and arrives at TADCASTER in time to secure a Conveyance to every part of the Kingdom by the Morning Coaches, and proceeds from thence by Sherburn to the PETRE's Arms, to SELBY, where it always arrives before the Sailing of the STEAM PACKETS for HULL, and waits at Selby until the Arrival of the Steam Packets from Hull, when Passengers, &c. are conveyed immediately back to Tadcaster, Knaresbro', Harrogate, &c.

Performed by WOOD, KIDD & POLLARD.

HULL, KNARESBRO', and HARROGATE
ELEGANT LIGHT
POST COACH.

THE Merchants, Traders, and Public in general, frequenting the Port of Hull, are most respectfully informed, that the "TRUE BLUE COACH" will commence running from the BAY HORSE INN, KNARESBROUGH, on MONDAY, the 5th of November, and on every *Monday, Thursday,* and *Saturday,* ensuing.

The TRUE BLUE will leave *Knaresbrough* at Five o'clock, and will pass through *Thorp-Arch* to *Tadcaster,* at which place it will arrive by Seven o'clock, in good time to meet the early morning Coaches to *London, Liverpool, Manchester, Leeds, York, Newcastle, Glasgow, Edinburgh,* and every part of the Kingdom.

The TRUE BLUE will proceed from *Tadcaster,* by way of *Sherburn,* to *Selby,* at which place it will arrive half an hour before the sailing of the PACKETS for *Hull.* At *Selby* the Coach will remain until the arrival of the Packets from *Hull,* when it will immediately return by the same Road to *Knaresbrough* and *Harrogate.*

The Proprietors anxious to afford every accommodation to the Public, rely with confidence, they will meet with support and patronage.

The Proprietors will not be accountable for any Box or Parcel above the value of Five Pounds, unless entered and paid for accordingly.　Performed by
ABBOTT, KIDD, and POLLARD.

October 31st, 1821.

Private coaches were hired to make connections to Selby Steam Packets.

Three

The Abbey

The Abbey Well c. 1700. The creation of a piped water supply to Selby in 1855 removed the need for the well. However, during the floods of 1892 the well was re-opened for use.

The Abbey Well today – a small rusty pipe at the bottom of a shed at the back of Wetherell's Department Store.

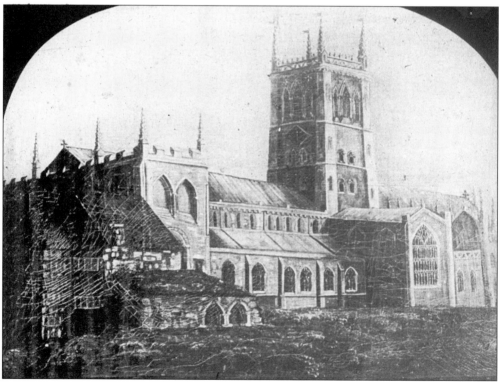

An etching of the Abbey showing the southern side.

The Abbey c. 1700.

The front
(west) view of
the Abbey
before the new
towers were
added in 1935.

A very rare view of restoration work that was carried out on the Abbey during 1891. To our modern eyes, the flimsy scaffolding looks too weak to hold a worker's weight.

Verger Kettlewell does not look amused at the mess created around the Abbey during the restoration work of 1891!

Canon Solloway and the Reverend Begby c. 1920. Canon Solloway came to Selby in 1910 as work was still being carried out on the Abbey following the great fire. He had some knowledge of architecture and oversaw all the work that was carried out for over thirty years including the completion of the Western towers in 1935. He retired in 1941 and is buried in the Abbey grounds.

The Abbey Gatehouse *c.* 1790. The Gatehouse with adjoining 'Middle Row' shops at this time extended right down the Market Place.

South West view of the Abbey *c.* 1800.

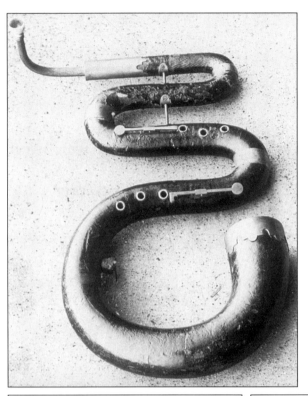

The Serpent c. 1900. This strange musical instrument was carved by a priest from Auxerre in 1590. This picture was probably taken at the Museum but after closure the Serpent was taken to the Abbey where it is now displayed. It was played by Mr Robinson at the 1827 Selby Musical Festival.

Introduction Programme for the Grand Music held at the Abbey 1827 and a list of the principal performers.

Selby Musical Festival,

1827.

FOR THE BENEFIT OF THE PUBLIC CHARITIES OF THE TOWN.

On THURSDAY, the 13th of SEPTEMBER,

WILL BE PERFORMED IN THE ABBEY CHURCH OF

SELBY,

A

GRAND SELECTION

OF

SACRED MUSIC,

FROM

THE CREATION, &c.

SELBY :

Printed by W. B. Gaby, &c. Market Place.

PRINCIPAL VOCAL PERFORMERS.

—o—

MISS FARRAR, MRS. AUSTIN,
Mr. BENNETT,
Mr. ISHERWOOD,
Mr. KAY, and Mr. ELLIS.

PRINCIPAL INSTRUMENTAL PERFORMERS.
Leader of the Band, ...Mr. WHITE
First Violin, Mr. Allan
Second Violin, Mr. Phillips
Viola, ..Mr. Hardman
Violoncello, ... Mr. Ivers
Double Bass, ... Mr. Wood
Bassoon, ... Mr. Dawson
Oboe, Mr. Wood
Flute, .. Mr. Foster
Clarionet, Mr. Walker
Horns, ... Messrs. Sugden and Creigg
Trumpets, .. Messrs. Clegg and Retalic
Alto Trombone, Mr. Young
Tenor Trombone, ... Mr. Bean
Bass Trombone, Mr. Hirst
Serpent, ... Mr. Robinson
Corno Bassetto, Mr. Moxon
Double Drums, Mr. Taylor
Organ,..................... Dr. CAMIDGE.

This old photograph of the Abbey Choir is displayed in the practice rooms above the War Memorial Chapel – the same room used by William Rawling for his lessons at the Blue Coat School.

The pulpit in the Abbey *c.* 1866. The gallery on the left was pulled down in the following year.

The Abbey Font is believed to have been part of the original Abbey Church sited at Church Hill. The decorative wooden cover was made in the fifteenth century and, according to legend, was intended to stop witches from stealing the baptism water for use in their magical potions.

A view of the altar, behind which is one of the wonders of the Abbey – the East Window.

A view toward the Eastern Nave *c.* 1890.

The carvings in the Abbey are a mixture of old and new. After the fire several pieces were lost and extensive restoration was required on those remaining.

The top of the Sedilia where notables can sit during ceremonies.

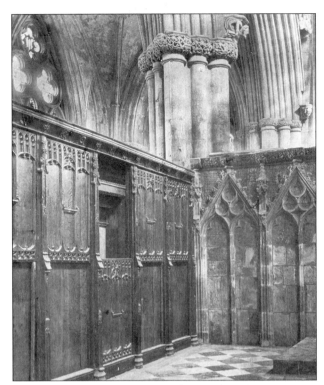

The internal panel work was completely destroyed during the fire. The only wooden structure saved was the decorative cover for the old Norman Font

Sunlight breaks through the window onto the south aisle *c.* 1890.

Verger Kettlewell stands in the ornate West Doorway c. 1890.

A Blue-coat school boy outside the West Entrance c. 1880. The boys were taught in the Scriptorium above the War Memorial Chapel and would enter through the Abbey West door. When travelling through some of the pupils would pull the alabaster from the walls.

The North
Door *c.* 1890.

A sketch drawing of the old
Abbey gatehouse. This sketch,
dated 1783, is held at the
Bodleian Library.

The old Abbey Tower that collapsed in 1690.

Overleaf: On the night of 19 October 1906 just before midnight Mr and Mrs Sykes were leaving the home of Mr and Mrs Brown when they saw flames in the windows of the Abbey. Mr A.L.C. Brown remembers that he was sent running over the Toll Bridge to collect the keys from the Verger, Christopher Bagshaw, whose house was on Barlby Bank. The town's fire engine arrived minutes later and a hose was connected to nearby stop-cock; three firemen held tight for the expectant gush of water which turned out to be a dribble. Only then was it realised that for conservation the town's water supply was turned off at night. Over twenty minutes were lost as a connection was re-established to the mains. During the next two hours the fire took hold watched by a bemused and shattered crowd. A fire engine arrived from York by train at two and from Leeds at three. The clock which had chimed the quarter hours throughout had stopped just before two but the most ominous sound came when the bells began to crash down into the destruction below.

The newspaper headlines were suitably sensational: 'A banquet for a Fire God'; 'When the clock stopped'. The *Selby Times* struck a more sombre note: 'Few people realised how deep-rooted was their love for the dear old Abbey until they saw it ruthlessly destroyed. Among the crowds who thronged the crescent many were sobbing bitterly'. However, despite the wreckage that remained, the fire became a catalyst for action. The Restoration Committee that was established soon reached their financial target of £40,000 and offers of help poured in from around the country. The fire re-established in the minds of Selebians the importance of the Abbey.

A strange fact also emerged after the fire (which may appeal to the superstitious). Important dates in the Abbey's history have featured the same numbers: the foundation (1069); the collapse of the Tower (1690); the fire (1906).

In 1887 Queen Victoria celebrated her Jubilee and the Abbey was suitably decked out in red, white and blue.

Queen Victoria's Jubilee 1887.

Four

Around and About

William Rawling not only took photographs of Selby but travelled further afield with his camera. This farmhouse, made from distinctive limestone, may be in the Monk Fryston area.

All Saints Church at Sherburn-in-Elmet *c.* 1900. Built on the site of an old Saxon Church dating from Athelstan's time the present church results from the accumulation of various architectural styles through the centuries. Inside the church are two halves of a Janus Cross – a relic that was divided after an ownership argument between the Vicar and the Warden.

An interior view of St Peter and St Paul Church at Drax. The church was constructed through the auspices of the Augustinian Priory which stood nearby and rumour insists that tunnels stretch from this site to the old Priory which would have allowed monks to rush valuables away during the Dissolution.

St Wilfrid's at Brayton with its fifteenth-century spire c. 1870.

The exact whereabouts of this Rawling photograph are not known but it depicts a play or pageant called 'The Suppression of a Nunnery'.

St Mary the Virgin Church in Hemingbrough. This picture was taken just after the restoration work of the Chancel under the architect Ewan Christian had been completed. The spire, which rises to 190 feet, was added in the fifteenth century under the auspices of Durham Priory.

Mrs Jones and her son, 'Stivvy', outside their old cottage, which was on the site of what was the Technical School, c. 1880. In the background is St James Church. On 10 May 1944 a Halifax bomber on exercise crashed into the spire killing the crew and several townspeople.

The site of Stivvy's cottage is now a car park. St James remains spireless.

Escrick Park *c.* 1900.

A man and his dog rest near a derelict cottage *c.* 1890.

William Rawling and friends on a walk *c*. 1892. Rawling is pictured centre with a white beard. The question remains open as to who took these pictures.

To our eyes, Edwardian clothing seems entirely unsuitable for a walk.

Barkisland
Hall, *c.* 1892.

The Selby
journalist
Addison Towse
accompanied
William
Rawling on his
visit to the
Hall. While
waiting for an
exposure on
one of his
photographic
plates Rawling
began to sing in
a deep bass
voice which
Towse claimed
'made the doors
rattle'.

A view down the river at Bolton Wood *c*. 1900.

A Selebians' trip to Fountains Abbey *c.* 1890. The two men to the far left are the brothers William and Robert Farley.

A Selebians' day out at Fountains Abbey *c.* 1892.

Selby Londesborough Rugby Football Club 1882-83. Those present for this picture were: Ben Connell, H. Eggleshaw, Ambrose Chambers, A. Nutt, J.H. Haynes, H. Stead, H. Firth,

W. Bowman, A.R. Swift, R. Conway, S. Walker, G. Winterbottom, C. Prost, A. Illingworth,
W. Drake, J.W. Haynes, W. Pulleyn, C. Earl, T. Haynes, D. Nutt.

A Cricket Club whist drive c. 1920.

The old windmill between Brayton and Selby *c.* 1880.

A Tennis Court laid out in the front of the only remaining part of Cawood Castle – the Gate House *c.* 1890.

The Gate House at Cawood Castle which was once the palace of the Archbishop of York and also home to Cardinal Wolsey.

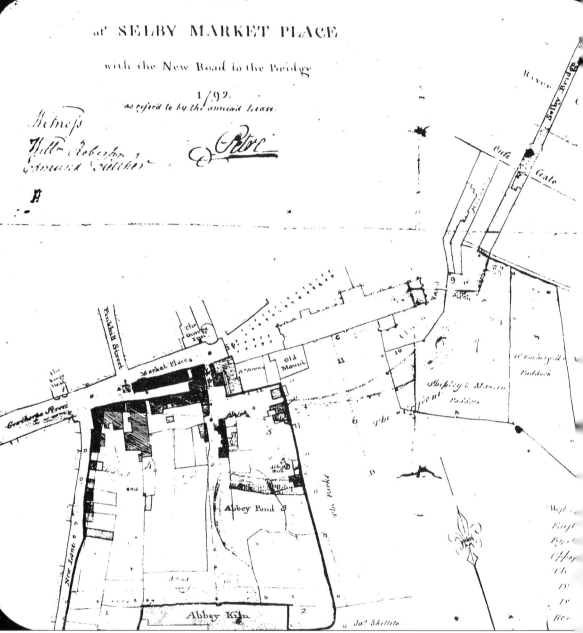

An old map of Selby Market Place. On this plan the Londesborough is listed as the 'George Inn'.